Cat Tales

Irma Sheppard
Karl Moeller

Acknowledgements and Copyright

Cover photo of Minnie © David A. Eastin

All other photos ©Karl Moeller or Irma Sheppard

ISBN-13
979-8-218-35233-2

Font Palatino

Book design by Karl Moeller
karl.moeller@me.com

**Front cover— Minnie: Don't Mess With Me
Back cover Sasha— Mister Mystic
Inside title page Max**

AMB Publishing resides in the hearts of man

All names and forms are the garbs and
covers under which the one life is hidden.

We should realize clearly that it is one life,
one light, which appears divided and
made into many by different shades.

Hazrat Inayat Khan

Sushi at home in Tucson

Dedication

To the memory of all the delightful cats we have loved

Karl's	**Irma's**
Mickey and son Oscar	Ginger
	Boots
	Tiger
Billy and Beau	Cativa
	Tzigana
Greycloud	WonTon
	Oedipus
Rocky	KittyKitty
	Sylvester
	Felix

Karma's shared cats

Sweetness
Sushi
Sam
Minnie and Max
ZemZem
Sasha

Bulletin and Kathy

Cat Tales

Sylvester and Felix

One day early in the summer of 1982, Sylvester came to us at Kathy's house in Norfolk, Virginia when the papergirl told twelve-year-old Pagan, "My mom said we can't keep him anymore. He's jumping around too much, breaking things—he broke a lamp yesterday and Mom said that was it—he'd have to go. Can you take him?" Pagan told her mom, and sight unseen, Kathy said yes. A cat-lover like me, Kathy was at home with cats. She already had one—Bulletin, Bully for short.

Sylvester arrived later with that day's paper. A handsome, long-legged tuxedo cat, he had no trouble making himself at home *toute suite*—and yes, he did jump around a lot, galloping from room to room, eating his bowl of kibble, trying out the sofa, then settling into the beanbag chair with Pagan. Bully and Sylvester spontaneously agreed to stay out of each other's way—a cat sensory negotiation that amazed and relieved us. Bully stayed mostly outside or in Kathy's bedroom and Sylvester stayed mostly inside. Kathy wasted no time in scheduling an appointment for Sylvester's neutering surgery. He weathered that in good cheer, and yes, he quieted down very sweetly, often lying between my arm and my torso as we napped together.

In July my thirteen-year-old son, Alex, came for a weeklong visit. While Kathy worked, Alex, Pagan and I spent a day on the Atlantic coast in Virginia Beach, hit the water slide and found other fun things to do. Alex loved cats and found Sylvester delightful. One day on an outing we came across a grey kitten for sale. It reminded us of the young grey cat I'd sent off with Alex when he went to live with his father in Pittsburgh. Alex and I agreed we should get this grey kitten, so we brought him home.

The next game was to name him. We settled on Felix, who scampered around and not surprisingly found Sylvester stretched out on the sofa. Felix clambered up to join him and immediately took to nursing on Sylvester's exposed nipple. Can you imagine the look of surprise on Sylvester's face?! On our faces too. Sylvester raised his head to check out what was happening, saw Felix sucking and kneading…and with that cat sensory communication, decided it was okay. I began to call him Uncle Sylvie.

From my room one day soon after this, I heard a truly strange, unearthly noise. Stepping into the living room, I saw Bully and Sylvester facing each other just a few feet apart, and Felix, totally alert, close behind his Uncle Sylvie. It was Sylvester making sounds I had never ever heard from a cat (or anyone) before. Or since. Sounds beyond hissing or growling—it was cat blasphemy—Sylvester warning Bully what he would do if he ever ever swatted or threatened little Felix again. This was beyond fatherhood. This was gangster talk! *I will squash your nose between my teeth… shred your eyeballs into spaghetti…bite off your tail and stuff it up your funky bum. Really? I will claw your belly to bits…rip your ears into windmills…*and more. Beyond cat opera!

And Bully, with each unearthly yowl, shrank further into a corner, too petrified to move a hair—crouched in silent terror. Sylvie on his tiptoes, fur all electric and sticking out. Neck stretched out at Bully daring any bit of squeak from him. Eyes promising brutal hell. Now low growls from between Sylvester's teeth—*get out and don't let me ever ever see you in here again.* Sylvester turned away, stalking tiptoe on stick straight legs, fur still at full attention. Sat next to Felix, turning his head away from the loathsome Bully, who slunk away out the back door.

Speechless, I blinked. Sylvester and Felix blinked. Sylvie started to wash Felix, wash the scare out of the little guy. Felix took it calmly, as a matter of course, sat with almost polite attention. Forever after, Bully came in to the house only once a day to eat, then scatted right back out.

Felix nursing on Sylvester

Karl welcomes Sweetness
to Tucson

Sweetness gets down to business

Sweetness, Sushi and Wiggy

In the spring of 1984, Sweetness, Karl's beautiful, longhaired calico
Persian cat flew in from Chicago, where she'd stayed with his father until
Karl settled in Tucson, Arizona. In order to fly, the weather had to be
neither too hot nor too cold in either place. When Karl picked her up at
the airport, he put his finger through the metal grill of her crate—though
she was groggy from sedation, she licked his finger in happy recognition.
A few months later she moved with us to Polly Lee's compound just
south of the Rillito River.

Sushi showed up in Polly's compound in 1985. Petite, black with a white
dot on her belly, six-months-old, sweet as pie. And pregnant! We
hesitated to challenge Sweetness with this young cat. Nearby in the
compound lived a Mexican family employed by Polly—Sushi (we hadn't
named her yet) had her two kittens under their trailer. They did their
best to take care of the little cat family and we helped with cat food. But
when Polly found out, she blew up and said they had to get rid of all the
cats—not trusting that they would or could take proper care of them?

Homes were found for the babies once they were six weeks old. The little
mom kept showing up on our patio and jumping into my lap. Karl
noticed how hard it was for me to resist her. One morning as he left for
work, he admonished me, "Don't you pet that kitty! Don't you let her up
in your lap!" I nodded and resisted temptation that day. When Karl came

"I picked her up."

home from work later, he came in the front door wearing a sheepish smile. In response to my inquiring eye, he said, "I petted the kitty. I picked her up. She'd started to stroke my leg as I stepped out of the car…"

We told Polly and the Mexican family that we would take the little mom in. Polly was fine with that. The teenage Mexican girls were sad of course, so I told them they could visit this sweet little black cat and still see her bouncing around the compound. Karl and I discussed names to no satisfactory agreement—it was our friend, John, who cut our hair, who said, "Why don't you just call her Sushi?" It stuck.

Sushi loved to play with Karl. He would call, "Sunbeam, Sushi!" and flash a light on a wall and she'd clamber up after it, intent on catching it and making it her own. She'd cuddle happily with either one of us, content as only a cat can be. But one day Karl noticed he was unaccountably fatigued and had a low-grade fever. Somehow Sushi had nicked Karl in play, scratched open a bit of skin. His doctor diagnosed this as cat scratch fever—it took him a few days to heal.

When Polly sold half of her compound to a real estate couple with a big dog, which they parked behind our bedroom window, we gave notice and bought our first house, taking Sweetness and Sushi with us. Sushi was so intent on staying with us that we found her lying on top of the last pile of stuff to be moved into our new home—she would not be left behind. We wondered then, if that was how it happened that she came wandering into this compound a while back…that she'd somehow been left behind.

Karl often played the piano in our living room and we began to notice that whenever he played Pete Townshend's "O Parvardigar" or the "Gujerati Arti," Sushi would lie under his chair on her back, belly up. As an experiment one day, I suggested he stop playing in the middle of one of these prayers. He did, and Sushi promptly rolled over and sat up. When Karl resumed playing the prayer, she immediately lay on her back again, paws up in the air as if in supplication. She perceived and took in Meher Baba's Love, which He had infused into these prayers. We shook our heads in wonder.

Karl playing for Sushi

Stephanie and Sweetness

In August 1987, my daughter Stephanie, twenty-one, came from Michigan to live with us. Stephanie loved cats and was happy to pet and play with Sweetness and Sushi. That fall Karl and I returned from a trip to Acapulco, Mexico. The staff of the grand hotel had left small gifts each evening on our pillows, including a colorful piñata shaped as a burro. We brought this home, eager to see what Sushi would make of it. They were about the same size. We set it on the floor and watched her stalk up to it, sniff it all over, including its butt. Oh! We wanted a photo of that—but how to get her to do that again? I dabbed butter on the burro's butt and camera ready, invited Sushi to sniff again. She did! Snap!

Sweetness passed on at age fifteen soon after we'd moved to the new place. Karl missed her. We talked about getting another cat, but realized that Sushi would not gracefully tolerate that. She was endlessly playful,

Sushi gets the burro's barcode

Sushi sniffing for corn

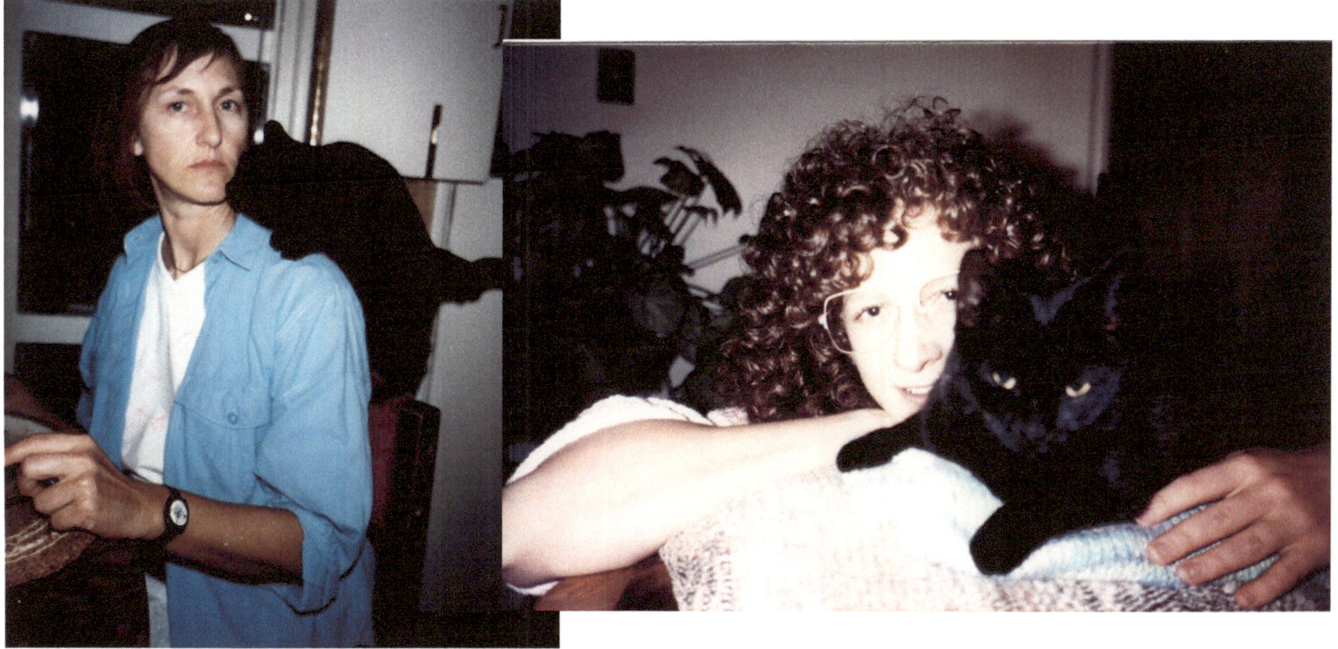

effortlessly cute and adventurous, wanting to taste everything we ate—chicken, steak, green beans, corn, etc. She was the most nearly perfect cat. We adored her. She 'owned' us. We told her, "In your next life you're gonna to be a dawg!"

Darling Sushi inside and out

Welcoming Wiggy

We decided it would be okay with Sushi if we had a rabbit—that the 'barcode' scent would be different enough to avoid competition. The rabbit would 'eat the backyard' —the various green things that grew haphazardly in our walled-in back yard. Then Karl wouldn't have to use the noisy weed-eater periodically to keep the growth down.

We found a handsome Chinchilla hare at the Humane Society and brought him home—Wiggy! He took to Sushi right away, but she snubbed him for some while. One day soon after Wiggy had arrived, I stepped out to the back patio to offer him some fresh lettuce leaves. "Wiggy! Wiggy!' I called. But it was Sushi who came—I'd called in my 'Sushi voice.' She sniffed at the lettuce…took a couple of bites…looked at me questioningly—you called me for this? I shrugged and laid the leaves in the shade of a shrub, out of the Tucson sun, figuring Wiggy would soon find them. When I came back out to see if he'd found them, what did I see?! Sushi lying on the lettuce leaves. Hers! No matter what.

Wiggy took to his job of eating the yard plus his bunny kibble with delight. He loved eating all the red pyracantha berries he could reach. He'd follow Karl around the back yard and race toward him when Karl cut some berries for him. When we let him in the house he'd go straight for Sushi's cat kibble, so we learned to put her food up on a counter when he was inside. Karl made the mistake of showing Wiggy how to use the cat door. He loved it… he'd pop in and after munching Sushi's kibble he'd find wires to chew on…whoops! That's no good…we had to put a barrier around the cat door outside in such a way that Sushi still had free access, though she had to jump up onto a low table and then down —Wiggy, of course, couldn't jump that high. We still had to watch him, though, when he was in the house—he'd go for wires in a flash. As we read the morning papers, we'd lift Wiggy up on the sofa next to us. His great joy there was to pull tissues out of the box, one at a time, dropping them on the sofa, not stopping until we removed the box from his reach.

Wiggy gets petted

Wiggy never lost his friendly interest in Sushi. He would chase her around the yard, then she would chase him—they both seemed to accept the give and take of play buddies. Maybe it helped that she stayed inside with us overnight—in fact slept in bed with us, while he slept outside. Wiggy grew into a large handsome bunny, bigger than Sushi, but she remained the boss.

One day I was brushing Wiggy on the low brick wall of the patio while Sushi lay sunning herself under the wooden swing. Aware of her presence, a mockingbird intent on protecting her nestlings, began to chit…chit… chit… her warning call. Wiggy, suddenly aware of the warning sounds in the air, hopped off the wall and around to where his good friend, Sushi, lay unsuspecting, unconcerned. Thumpthumpthump went Wiggy's hind leg—warning her of imminent danger! Unaware that she herself was the danger!

Sushi and the swing

Stephanie and Sushi

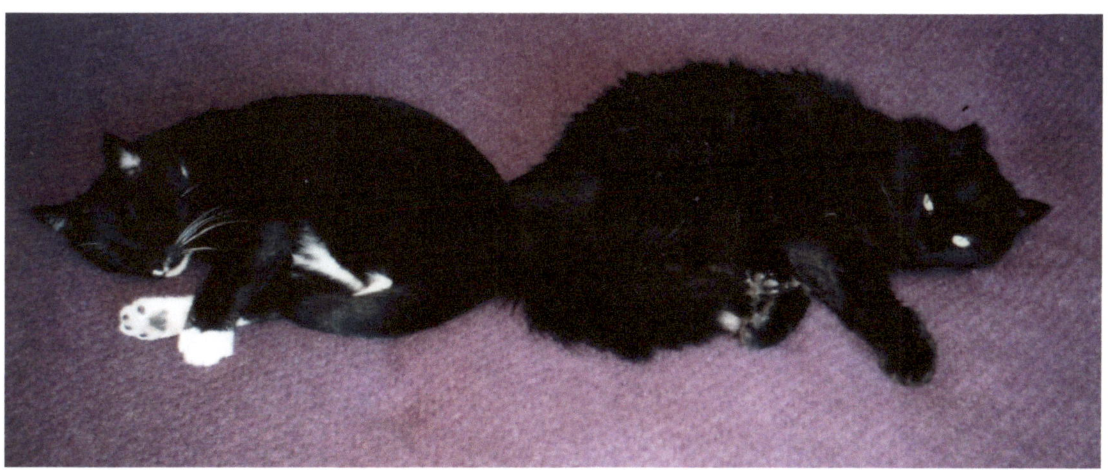

Minnie and Max

"Would you be willing to take my two cats for two months? My daughter and I are leaving for Guatemala for two months tomorrow morning. The receptionist at Dr. Peters' office said you might be willing to take them… if you won't take them, I'll have to take them to the Humane Society." It was about a month since we'd finally let Sushi go, and we still missed her. " Yes. Yes, of course we'll take your two cats for two months.

She came a half hour later with the brother and sister cats in a carrier, plus a large bag half full of cat food. "They've been vaccinated, neutered and spayed. They were born on the Tohono O'odham Reservation seven months ago." She told me their names, but I already knew I'd rename them. She opened the carrier and the two cats streamed out, immediately exploring the house, sniffing everything, looking like fish weaving through water.

"What if we get attached to them?" "That's okay—I'd have to find new homes for them when we get back anyway." "Call us when you return so you can come and see them." "No," she said, "it's hard enough to leave them now." And she left…no lingering.

The male had medium long fur, all black with a big white dot at the tip of his tail. She'd called him Prince, so he became 'the black cat formerly known as Prince.' His sister was a black and white tuxedo kitty, with a

white Charlie Chaplin moustache. I knew her name immediately—
Minnie. It took me two whole days before I figured it out— if she was
Minnie, he had to be Max! They may have been born on the reservation
just west of Tucson, but they spoke regular cat—Minnie with a strong
Siamese accent—better to boss Max with.

They took to the cat door like fish to water. And thus met Wiggy, our
resident Chinchilla hare. Sniff sniff…sniff sniff… Minnie and Wiggy
became fast friends, while Max and Wiggy eyed each other warily from a distance. Males! M&M were handsome, healthy, hungry, happy to get petted. Yet for almost a year, deep in our minds and hearts, they were 'not Sushi.'

Two years later we moved to a sort of duplex—two houses with a common wall, so Karl's father could come from Chicago and live by us in the smaller house. We installed a cat door leading to the narrow

Amy and Minnie

walled in rose garden out front. M&M could leap up and over the walls if
they wanted and soon did. They decided they wanted to walk with us in
the evenings. We'd stand at the back door saying, "Kitty walk! Kitty
walk!" and they'd show up in seconds. We'd walk two blocks south and
two west, as M&M roamed the front yards we passed, sniffing the kitty
newspaper. At the second block west, we'd rest a bit while M&M scoured
the neighborhood for cat-worthy news. After several minutes I'd clap and

M&M on either side of a sliding glass window

call their names. They'd come running and we'd head for home. We never met a dog on these walks—lucky for any dog. When I wanted to take a longer walk, I had to close the cat door before I changed into my walking shoes—if Minnie saw me do that, she'd run out the cat door in a flash—didn't want to be left behind. She was a smarty!

After five years there, we moved to a handsome adobe brick ranch house in the foothills just north of Tucson. We spent an unmentionable amount of money to replace the wobbly fence around what had been a dog yard, and was about to be a cat yard, adjoining our own backyard. We added three feet of diamond wire to the cinderblock wall in back, so we had eight feet of fencing all around, and a T-section on top of all that to keep coyotes and bobcats out, and M&M in. It didn't work. Minnie smelled the previous owners' pitbull, especially in the now cat yard, and managed to escape every evening after dusk. I'd find her in the morning across the road, hiding in a neighbor's yard. She outsmarted Karl for five months, no matter how he tried to keep her in. A friend told him he'd used a low voltage electric wire to keep his Jack Russell in, so Karl installed such a wire around the top of the cat yard fence. Minnie got out again that night…and never again!

During one summer monsoon thunderstorm, a big dog showed up on the driveway across the front of the house, wet and shivering. I quickly enclosed M&M in our bedroom, while Karl let this dog in. We dried her off a bit and found a phone number on her dog tag, called and left a message. Not long after, her human came, explaining how thunder freaked his dog, Mattie, into jumping over their wall. When I released M&M later, they sniffed the dog scent in the hall, and never forgot it. Weeks later, Mattie showed up again though it was not storming. Karl put her in into a fenced in area between the house and his studio. The dog paced the L-shaped area…back and forth…while M&M watched closely from our sliding doors—their heads wagging back and forth to match his pacing. Suddenly Minnie flashed out the cat door— the dog had pushed open the gate to the back yard. I rushed out to protect her. When I got there, Minnie was *hissing, hissing,* having backed this big dog into a corner and into a rose bush, where she was whining and crying. I picked her up and locked her in the house. Soon after, his human came for her once again. We never saw Mattie again.

In spite of all our efforts, we could not make our back yard totally safe from occasional bobcat intrusions. There was desert immediately behind our back wall, and our front yard was desert too—in fact the whole neighborhood lay in the desert. Our cats, as well as our pool, were most likely the main attractions for bobcats to try to get in. There was a tall pine in front of the house, which bobcats could climb to get on the roof,

Minnie: "I can be sweet, too."

and from there, jump down into the back yard. The first time this happened, Minnie dashed out the cat door intent on dealing with the intruder, who was frantically jumping up trying to clear the T-section. Unsuccessfully. I ran to retrieve Minnie before the bobcat could maul her. I caught up to her as she, in full catfight mode, hissed and stretched claws out at the bobcat, which was at least three times her size.

At Minnie's insistent threats, the bobcat sprang up the wall—literally climbing the wall until it reached the T-section, then came down again… only to risk Minnie's hissing claws…so he climbed up again…and down …and on they went like this all across the back wall…until the poor bobcat reached the Texas Ranger hedge, where it found enough traction to jump over the wall into the desert. I had followed them, never needing to 'rescue' Minnie. She now turned back toward the house, pumped up, almost prancing in full glory. Max had been backup all along, right behind me.

This was the last time Minnie bullied a bobcat. This had taken something out of her, a ten-year-old cat now. She slept more from now on. Karl wrapped barbed wire around the trunk of the pine out front, so bobcats couldn't climb it any more. But the heat pump behind Karl's studio still allowed easy jumps up onto the roof. We also heard that bobcats could easily jump eight feet or more straight up to the roof. This was desert life.

Minnie's growly Siamese voice enhanced her bossy habits, not just over mild-mannered Max, but over me too. Well, I wasn't having it. Often when I was in the kitchen, she'd come in, demanding some of whatever I was preparing or she wanted her 'tea time treat' right now! *Mrroww! Mrroww!*

One time, knowing she hated to be picked up, I said to her, "I'll pick you up." *Mrroww! Mrroww!* She insisted. "I'll pick you up." *Mrroww! Mrroww…* as if she didn't care. I picked her up…she twisted and turned and pushed her paws at me. After a moment I set her down. *Mrroww! Mrroww!* "I'll pick you up." Silence. Minnie collected herself, sat with paws put neatly together, didn't move. I never had to say that to her again. When she wanted her food or treat, she'd sit demurely on the floor near their food dishes…and quietly wait. Truly a 'tidy' cat!

Though confined to the back yards, M&M were good hunters, perhaps because they'd been born on the Reservation. They caught and brought into the house a medley of creatures: birds, especially white wing doves, who tended to be slow, packrats, kangaroo rats, lizards of all colors and sizes, a couple of bats, one white dead scorpion and one snake. As I entered my study one morning, I saw a small snake lying motionless on the rug, about two feet from the cat door. M&M sat or lay nearby, unconcerned, washing themselves. The snake had a bite in its lower end. It lay still and I wondered if it was dead. It wasn't a rattler, but I didn't know what kind of snake it was, so I got my snake book to try to identify it. Suddenly it began to move.

I dropped the book and went to wake Karl. "There's a snake in my study!" Groggy, he got up. Max was sniffing at the snake now. I shooed

him away. "I know you're quick, but a snake can bite you too, and if it does, we're not going to spend a thousand dollars to save you!" He must have gotten the message because I never found another snake in the house. I figured this was Max's doing because Minnie would have killed the snake and eaten some or all of it. Karl picked the snake up with a rake and deposited it in our front desert yard.

Whenever we saw Minnie or Max come in with some creature in their mouths, we would shout, *"Out! Out!!"* Minnie would turn right around and take her catch out and eat it there. Max would simply drop what he had in his mouth and look at us, as if pleased to have brought us a gift. If the creature were dead or injured we'd put it out in the front desert. If it was alive and well, we'd soon be frantically moving furniture trying to catch it.

M&M liked to be with us in the living room, Minnie favoring Karl, sliding herself neatly between his left leg and his armchair, enjoying his loving pets. She also liked to lie on the back of his armchair, just behind his neck, facing me so she could keep a watchful eye on not just me, but also the desert out the front window. One never knew who might be passing along the driveway: rabbits, coyotes, javelinas, roadrunners, doves, lizards, Gambel's quail babies trailing their mom, tarantulas or even Gila monsters.

Minnie and Max, seventeen years old, passed on about a month apart by January 2014. We took a break before taking on loving a new cat. We went on the "Four Pillar" pilgrimage in Italy and Spain: St. Francis in Assisi, Meher Baba in Portofino, Jesus and Baba in Venice, St. Teresa and John of the Cross in Avila, Spain. We started out in Rome, saw Pope Francis give his Sunday address to the public in St. Peter's Square. Never in my life had I thought I would ever see a pope—I was pleased that it was this one.

Young ZemZem and Sasha en route from Virginia to Tucson, 2011, prior to coming to us

ZemZem and Sasha

Home in Tucson once again, we felt ready to welcome a new cat. Karl searched Craig's List for a young, black, shorthaired female and found her…offered with a shorthaired tabby tuxedo male. They needed a new home—theirs had become overcrowded with a new premature baby and a male husky. Their folks had brought these cats along from Virginia when they'd moved to Tucson. We visited and fell in love with the female—I had already picked out a name for her—ZemZem—the name of the well in the Arabian desert, to which an angel had directed Hagar, to satisfy her son, Ishmael's thirst. This well is still on the site that includes the Kaaba in Mecca, the place of worship for Muslim pilgrims.

The male cat was sweet and friendly, stroking Karl's leg immediately, but looked frankly moth-eaten—strips of fur were missing on his back and the back of his hind legs were bald. His folks just shrugged and looked blank when we asked about that. Whatever it was, it hadn't affected ZemZem. They were about two years old and had grown up together, but were not siblings. After a brief hesitation, we agreed to take them both. The young couple breathed sighs of relief. Somehow I already knew the male cat's name—Sasha, the popular nickname for Alexander in Russian.

Cat naps

ZemZem and
Sasha in Tucson

ZemZem was extraordinarily sweet and cuddly. A long, thin black cat, she'd stretch out on my arm as we watched a movie at home. I made separate beds for them in the living room. I'd see Sasha in his bed licking more fur off his back. I'd go to him, singing, "Sasha Baby…Sasha Buddha…Sasha Baba…" This got his attention—he'd stop licking and jump off the sofa and I'd give him a small treat. Soon he stopped the frantic licking and in a few months his fur grew back—now he looked healthy and handsome. We figured he hadn't felt safe around the male husky.

After ZemZem and Sasha had been with us for a couple of months, we invited their former folks for tea, and a chance for them to see how comfortable the cats had become in our back yard. We sat on the back patio, overlooking the pool, the desert, the Catalina

Mountains…Sasha stayed sitting by the rosemary bush on the far side of the pool and ZemZem stayed sitting on the diving board. They made no effort, after initial greetings, to nuzzle up to this couple for old times sake. Maybe they smelled of husky? And no longer housebound, the cats loved their new back yard freedom. Cats do.

One day Karl and I heard a commotion a bit before dusk. Rushing out, we saw a bobcat chasing ZemZem. We ran to rescue her and Sasha rushed out with us. We got to ZemZem, but not before the bobcat had slashed her cheek. Karl opened a gate and the bobcat bolted out into the desert, chased by Sasha—Karl shut the gate before Sasha got out. We took ZemZem to be treated that evening and brought her home, a protective cone around her head.

Karl and Sasha

Perhaps it was the strange cone—I don't know—but something changed between her and Sasha. They no longer napped together—ZemZem began to seek high up spots—sitting on top of a bookcase, climbing our clothes to get to the highest shelf in the closet. One early morning in August 2015, as I stepped out the front door to get the paper, I spotted ZemZem in the driveway, stalking a bird. How did she get out?? I called and she came inside with me. The next morning I found her on the front drive again, and again she happily came in with me. The next morning, she was gone. Gone! We never saw her again. Perhaps it was a coyote… so sad…she had been so sweet.

ZemZem and Irma

Now we had only Sasha, who continued to be handsome and also sweet in his own dog-like kind of way.

In the spring of 2015 Karl and I realized we had to leave our beautiful foothills home (leave Tucson!?), though we'd always thought to live here for the rest of our lives. Initially we saw the compelling issues as money and eventually, water. It was only after we'd settled in Asheville, North Carolina that we realized that the process of participating in three pilgrimages—Beads-on-One-String all over India with Don Stevens and twenty-two Baba lovers in 2010; the Heartland Pilgrimage from Charlotte, NC to Prague, Oklahoma and back to Myrtle Beach, SC with Jill English and twelve Baba lovers in 2013; and the Four Pillar Pilgrimage in Italy and Spain with three Baba lovers in 2014—that all these pilgrimages had made changes within us that we had not been fully conscious of—including the ability to detach from this lovely home. Karl said, "Where will we move to?" "Asheville," I said. For decades I'd heard that this or that Baba lover lived in Asheville, this or that one had moved to Asheville, and friends who were not Baba lovers had visited and raved about Asheville. That November we visited Ken and Debby Blackman, Tucson Baba lover friends who had moved to Asheville. Ken took us to Baba meetings, where we met people we knew and some we didn't. We decided to move to Asheville—the large and growing Baba community there was the vital draw.

We went home and made arrangements to sell our home. People began to come to see our house. Sasha helped me greet them as they arrived. I took them through and around to the back yard, mentioned the resort across the desert that put on tremendous firework displays for Memorial Sunday and New Year's Eve, the horse and hiking trails we had access to, five fruit trees and the rose garden in the back yard. It was Sasha who led us from one room to the next, as if to say…and look at this room…and this room…leading us out to Karl's studio and the laundry room. When the people left, Sasha sat washing himself, as if congratulating himself on a job well done.

We were nervous about having our house re-appraised—some months earlier an appraiser had given us a figure below that which we'd paid for the house. When the new appraiser came in, Sasha went right to him, was greeted warmly and petted. The man said, "What a sweet cat…my old cat just died recently…I still miss her." Sasha continued to welcome him. It felt like a good sign. I handed the appraiser a long list of 'intangibles'—features of our house and property that made it more desirable. He took it and thanked me. I left him to proceed. He worked at his appraisal for several hours, handed the list back to me, petted Sasha again and left. A few days later we heard from the prospective buyers' real estate agent that he had appraised our home for over $60,000 more than what we had paid for it. This meant that the couple could afford to buy it and that we'd have enough money to buy a home in Asheville outright, with no mortgage—neither of us would have to get a job.

The day before we departed, I had the housecleaning crew give the empty house a final cleaning. We'd planned a farewell lunch with a few neighbors at a nearby restaurant. Before leaving I put Sasha and his food and water outside the cat door, feeling that the back yard was safe, and so he and the cleaning crew wouldn't tangle. When we returned an hour or so later—he was gone! Nowhere in the back yard. We called and called. How did he get out? He'd never gone out before. We had to go sign final papers, after which we returned to search and call again. We called from every part of the acre of property…we called and called…it was 105 degrees in mid-May…every time I thought it was too hot to stand and call out in the sun, I'd think about Sasha in the desert, unable to survive —coyotes, bobcats, no water…so I'd call some more…for close to an hour. In final despair I returned to the back yard.

Karl and I had agreed to say the "Beloved God" prayer by the back gate before we left our beautiful home. We stood by the north gate. With a heavy heart I closed my eyes. Suddenly I heard the rustle of leaves…and Karl said, *"Look!"* I opened my eyes to see Sasha racing around the pool toward us! Oh Baba! He came to us and we petted and fussed over him, all our hearts uplifted. With true fervor we said the prayer… carried Sasha to our fully packed Honda Element…and drove off without the slightest hint of regret for leaving this lovely foothills home—we were so overjoyed to have Sasha safely with us. Why had he left the back yard? Did he go looking for us? We spent one last night in Tucson at the home of a friend. The next day, as we prepared to leave, I found Sasha lying in my bag! *"I'm going with you. Don't leave me!"*

Our four-day, 2,000 mile road trip to Asheville, North Carolina was uneventful—Sasha took all the changes in stride, sleeping on a pillow in the well between our

Don't leave me!

En route to Asheville

car seats. On our first night in a motel, before we went out for dinner, Karl moved a chair into the bathroom and put his slippers on the chair. Sure enough, we came back to find Sasha installed on top of Karl's slippers—safe in their comfy and familiar scent.

Our next challenge was to make ourselves as comfortable as possible in a two-room basement walkout in Asheville. We kept Sasha inside for the first week, then I'd go out with him, letting him explore the back garden as I kept close to him. He learned and obeyed my "No!" when he ventured toward the fenced edges of the yard. In this apartment Sasha learned to drink from the drizzling tap of the bathroom sink—a habit that took years to break—success finally came with a kitty water fountain and our stony insistence. During his years with us in Tucson, Sasha had drunk only from our swimming pool, which twice led to his falling in (we presume) and coming in the house dripping wet—he didn't seem to mind.

Early in August 2016, we moved into our new home—our retirement cottage, as we call it. We had cat doors installed in the back door and in the screen door on the enclosed deck. After a week of being housebound again, we let Sasha out. Soon he was experiencing a few challenges to his right of domain—male cats next door and across the street and at least one groundhog precipitated yowls, squawks and slashing claw fights at the outer cat door. Eventually it settled down as Sasha masterfully defended his territory.

We took him to a vet referred to us, Dr. Amber, for check up and booster shots. As Sasha sat acquiescent on the examination table, she exclaimed, "Oh, what a handsome cat you are!" I said, "We think he's handsome… do you say this to all the cats?" "Oh no!" she said. "If he were a guy, I'd hit on him!" Wow! Yes, Sasha truly is handsome.

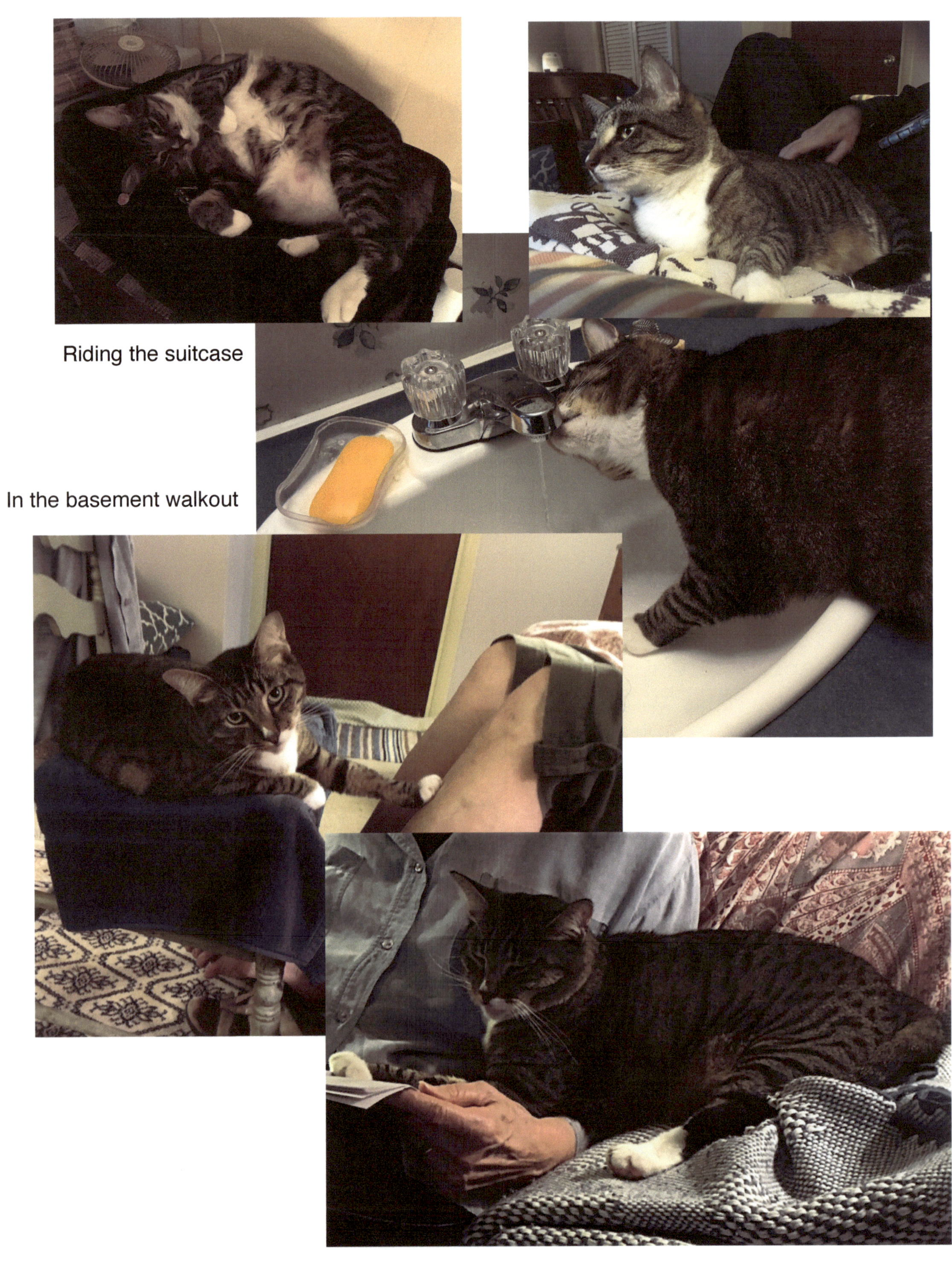

Riding the suitcase

In the basement walkout

Early days in Asheville
in the back garden

I took a photo of Sasha as he lay stretched out on an oriental rug. Karl sent the photo to be made into a jigsaw puzzle. Between all his stripes and the intricate pattern on the rug, it was the most difficult jigsaw puzzle I'd ever put together—it took weeks.

Sasha learned the sounds of tea preparations around 4 P.M. each day—that was when he gets his teatime treat. So he shows up in the kitchen and sits in front of his dish waiting patiently for me to put his treat into his bowl. He learned the word 'treat' and a few other words—brush, lie down, water, drink, walk, outside—so well that we have to spell some of them in order not to arouse his desire.

He joins me for early morning walks in the neighborhood, running alongside me, scooting under a car or a shrub when he hears a car coming, spraying car tires and bumpers, bushes, trash by the roadside—marking it all as his. He only comes five or six houses down the block with me, then occupies himself with sniffing,

Posing for posterity in our retirement cottage

Taking Meher Baba's darshan

spraying or hiding if the birds become raucous, warning us away from their nests. When I return, he comes running out to meet me and happily leads the way home.

In the early evenings these days, we put our plates full of dinner on tray tables and watch movies on our big screen. Sasha snuggles in next to me in my armchair. I pet him…and he looks at me, slowly shutting his eyes… opens them and slowly

Sasha says, "I love you."

shuts them again. I heard that this is a way that cats express love—so I return the slow shutting of eyes to him—we do this, back and forth, for a minute or so…I love you…I love you…I love you…and of course his purring becomes deeper and louder … and we both bliss out.

I was sitting in my armchair one day, with Sasha lying asleep on the arm, facing to the back. I was thinking about a phrase that had come up in a reading meeting the day before: *speak to the soul*. Yes, I thought, speak to the best part of someone, *speak to the soul*. Noticing Sasha, I thought, yes, even a kitty soul. *No, it's not a kitty soul…it's a soul!* (just as mine is). I hadn't moved or made a sound, but in that instant, Sasha raised his head and looked at me, eye to eye… and he did not look away. He had taken in what I had thought! My thought had connected with his soul. And from his soul he responded.

At home with Sasha

Guarding the back deck

SuperCat!

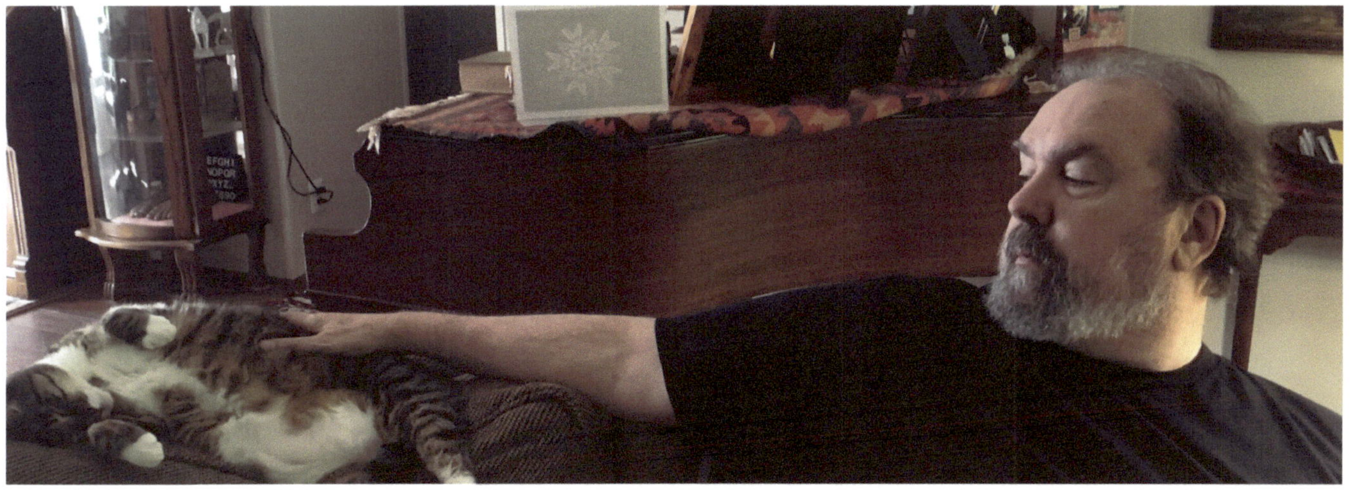

Sasha continues to enjoy life with us in Asheville.

Cats from 8 to 80

Effortless grace, beauty, strength, agility, playfulness and endless curiosity, repose and quietude, eventual trust and close companionship

Ginger, Boots Tiger, Cativa, Tzigana, WonTon, Oedipus, KittyKitty, Sylvester, Felix, Sweetness, Sushi, Sam, Minnie, Max, ZemZem, Sasha.

My mother called me *Katzenmutter*—Catmother, and I am.

Cats speak to me visually as much or more than orally.

Through the decades I have learned, cat by cat, the rules of optimal cohabitation. The secret is love.

—Irma

Loving Cats

Thinking about the cats I've lived with since I was a boy—whether they were relaxed and sleepy, mischevious and playful, young or growing old, two things remain true over the years—I always wish I'd been a better human companion. I have gotten better. And—every single cat was the best and most lovable companion I could have ever asked for.

My beloved cats, I love you all and I always will.

—Karl

Asheville January 2024